Applying the Standards: Evidence-Based Reading
Grade 4

Credits
Content Editor: Kristina L. Biddle
Copy Editor: Elise Craver

Visit *carsondellosa.com* for correlations to Common Core, state, national, and Canadian provincial standards.

Carson-Dellosa Publishing, LLC
PO Box 35665
Greensboro, NC 27425 USA
carsondellosa.com

ISBN 1-4838-1462-9
02-243151151

Table of Contents

Introduction

The purpose of this book is to engage students in close reading while applying the standards. The Common Core reading and language strands are reflected in the interactive questions that follow each passage.

The lessons are intended to help students not only comprehend what they read superficially, but also to help them read complex texts closely and analytically. Students need to get involved deeply with what they are reading and use higher-order thinking skills to reflect on what they have read.

On the following activity pages, students will read a variety of literature and informational passages. These are brief but lend themselves to more complex thinking. Given the opportunity to study shorter texts, students can better practice the higher-level skills they need to closely read more demanding texts.

Each selection is followed by text-dependent questions. Students are prompted to pay attention to how a text is organized, to solve the question of why the author chose specific words, to look for deeper meaning, and to determine what the author is trying to say.

Use the included rubric to guide assessment of student responses and further plan any necessary remediation. The art of close reading is an invaluable skill that will help students succeed in their school years and beyond.

Common Core Alignment Chart

Use this chart to plan your instruction, practice, or remediation of a specific standard. To do this, first choose your targeted standard; then, find the pages listed on the chart that correlate to the standard.

Common Core State Standards*		Practice Pages
Reading Standards for Literature		
Key Ideas and Details	4.RL.1–4.RL.3	5–7, 9–11, 13–16, 18, 19, 21–24, 26, 28
Craft and Structure	4.RL.4–4.RL.6	5, 7, 9–11, 13–15, 18, 19, 21, 23, 24, 26
Integration of Knowledge and Ideas	4.RL.7, 4.RL.9	6, 16, 28
Range of Reading and Level of Text Complexity	4.RL.10	Each reading passage can be adapted to exercise this standard.
Reading Standards for Informational Text		
Key Ideas and Details	4.RI.1–4.RI.3	29–31, 33, 35, 36, 38, 40, 42–44, 46–48, 50–55, 57, 59–62
Craft and Structure	4.RI.4–4.RI.6	29, 31, 33, 35, 40, 42, 44, 46–48, 50–52, 54, 55, 59, 62
Integration of Knowledge and Ideas	4.RI.7–4.RI.9	29, 30, 33, 35, 36, 38, 40, 42–44, 46–48, 51, 52, 54, 55, 57, 59–62
Range of Reading and Level of Text Complexity	4.RI.10	Each reading passage can be adapted to exercise this standard.
Reading Standards: Foundational Skills		
Fluency	4.RF.4	Each reading passage can be adapted to exercise this standard.
Language Standards		
Conventions of Standard English	4.L.1–4.L.2	5, 28
Knowledge of Language	4.L.3	6, 18, 21, 23, 28, 60
Vocabulary Acquisition and Use	4.L.4–4.L.6	6, 7, 9–11, 13, 14, 18, 19, 21, 26, 28, 31, 40, 42, 44, 46–48, 50, 52–54, 57, 59, 61

Reading Comprehension Rubric

Use this rubric as a guide to assess students' written work. It can also be offered to students to help them check their work or as a tool to show your scoring.

4	_____ Offers insightful reasoning and strong evidence of critical thinking _____ Makes valid, nontrivial inferences based on evidence in the text _____ Skillfully supports answers with relevant details from the text _____ Gives answers that indicate a complete understanding of the text _____ Gives answers that are easy to understand, clear, and concise _____ Uses conventions, spelling, and grammar correctly
3	_____ Offers sufficient reasoning and evidence of critical thinking _____ Makes inferences based on evidence in the text _____ Supports answers with details from the text _____ Gives answers that indicate a good understanding of the text _____ Gives answers that are easy to understand _____ Uses conventions, spelling, and grammar correctly most of the time
2	_____ Demonstrates some evidence of critical thinking _____ Makes incorrect inferences or does not base inferences on evidence in the text _____ Attempts to support answers with information from the text _____ Gives answers that indicate an incomplete understanding of the text _____ Gives answers that are understandable but lack focus _____ Gives answers containing several errors in conventions, spelling, and grammar
1	_____ Demonstrates limited or no evidence of critical thinking _____ Makes no inferences _____ Does not support answers with details from the text _____ Gives answers that indicate little to no understanding of the text _____ Gives answers that are difficult to understand _____ Gives answers with many errors in conventions, spelling, and grammar

Name _____

Read. Then, answer the questions.

Mike and Moe

We chose our first cat, Mike, at the animal shelter when he was only eight weeks old. He was a very independent kitten from the beginning.

When Mike was about two years old, I heard a faint cry while I was reading on the patio. I did not see anything. The crying persisted. Finally, about 10 feet above where I was sitting, I saw a tiny kitten sitting on a tree branch.

I called for my brother, Ben, to bring a ladder. Ben climbed up the first two rungs and handed me the tiniest kitten I had ever seen.

The kitten did not have a collar, so we did not know who he belonged to. But, we knew that the kitten needed special care, so we took the kitten to our veterinarian. She told us how to feed him with an eyedropper.

When we got home, Ben took a picture of the kitten and hung it on a telephone pole. We wanted to take care of him, but if his owner was looking for him, she might be sad or upset. Ben and I fed the kitten with an eyedropper for two weeks. Nobody claimed him, so we named him Moe.

At first, Mike was not nice to Moe. Now, they are good friends. We have no idea how Moe ended up in that tree, but we are glad that he did. We think that Mike is glad too.

1. How long do the brothers need to feed the kitten with an eyedropper?

_____

2. Is the story told in first- or third-person narration? Circle the evidence in the story that supports your answer.

_____

3. Why do the brothers hang a picture of the kitten on a telephone pole? Use evidence from the story to support your answer.

_____

_____

 **Reflect**

How does the author support the fact that Ben and his brother are caring?

_____

_____

_____

_____

Name _____

Read. Then, answer the questions.

The Girl and the Almonds

A girl, hungry after a day of play, spied a jar of honeyed almonds. "Mom, may I please have some nuts?" she asked, her **ravenous** tummy growling.

"It's almost time for dinner," said her mother. "Only take a handful."

The greedy little girl reached into the jar, grabbing as many nuts as she could hold. But, when she tried to pull out her hand, it got stuck. She tugged until her arm grew sore and tears of disappointment flowed down her cheeks.

Amazed at her daughter's stubbornness, her mother said, "Let go of half of the almonds, or you will end up with none at all."

The Raven and the Pitcher

For months, rain had not fallen in the desert. The cacti's fleshy leaves had dried and withered into flat, leathery discs. Creeks shaded by the canyons had turned to clay.

A raven circled high above. He knew that death would come by sunset if he could not find water. Spotting something in a deserted campsite, the raven swooped down. It was a pitcher half-filled with water! But, he could not reach the water.

He perched beside the container and thought. Grabbing a small pebble, he dropped it into the pitcher. He dropped pebble after pebble into the pitcher, and the water rose closer to the top. At last, he was able to drink his fill and save his life.

1. What does *ravenous* mean in "The Girl and the Almonds"?

_____

2. The daughter is stubborn. What evidence in the story supports this?

_____

_____

3. Read the first paragraph of "The Raven and the Pitcher." Why did the author include such descriptive language?

_____

_____

 Reflect

The fables have similar themes. Compare and contrast the two stories using evidence from both to support your answer.

_____

_____

Name _____

Read. Then, answer the questions.

The Milkmaid and Her Pail

A young milkmaid walked down a dusty path with a pail of fresh, warm cow's milk poised upon her head. As she neared her small, thatched-roof hut, daydreams filled her mind.

"The milk was so creamy this morning," she thought. "I'll churn the cream into golden butter that I will sell at the village market tomorrow. With the money I make from the butter, I will buy a dozen eggs, and from the dozen eggs will hatch a dozen chickens. The dozen chickens will each lay a dozen eggs, and then I will have chickens, eggs, and butter to sell at the Autumn Fair."

"With the money I make at the fair, I will buy a silver gown **embellished** with pearls. This winter, I will wear it to the Sheriff's Ball. When his son sees me, he'll seek me to dance. But, will I? Oh, never! As he begs to take my hand, I'll sweetly smile and shake my head from side to side like this!"

In that moment, the milkmaid's dreams turned back to reality. The wooden pail lay broken on the ground. In the end, she had nothing, not even the milk she started with.

1. What does *embellished* mean?

_____

2. What is the central message of the story?

_____

_____

3. How does the author support the central message?

_____

_____

☀ Reflect

In the end, the milkmaid is left with even less than she started with. How would the central message of the story be affected if she still had some milk left? Why?

_____

_____

_____

_____

Name _____

Read. Then, answer the questions on page 9.

Learning to Fly

The Metro train **whisked** to a stop deep beneath the US capital. Roberto was so excited that he had to remind himself to breathe. Two years ago, he and his family emigrated from Mexico to a small town in northern Utah. His father was a missile scientist who worked for NASA (National Aeronautics and Space Administration). He was developing new rockets for a space airplane that would someday replace the space shuttle.

As far back as Roberto could remember, he wanted to be a US Air Force pilot. He won a writing contest with an essay titled "Why I Want to Be an Air Force Pilot." The prize was an all-expenses-paid trip to Washington, DC, with his family. Today, he was on his way to visit the National Air and Space Museum.

"Hang on, Maria," he said, grasping his sister's hand. The escalator rose steeply toward the morning light.

The Air Force cadet who was **escorting** the family explained the subway. "Almost 30 years ago the first subway began running under the city," he said. "The subway averages more than half a million riders each workday. This has reduced pollution from car fumes. The exhaust was harming the marble and granite on the monuments."

When they arrived at the National Air and Space Museum, Roberto was overwhelmed. At the F-16 exhibit, the cadet described what it felt like to fly faster than the speed of sound. When Roberto did not think that he could handle the excitement anymore, the cadet asked him if he wanted to fly in a simulator. With the cadet as his wingman, Roberto shakily raised the computerized airplane off the ground and into the air. It was an intense experience that left Roberto **exhilarated**.

Seven hours later, the family returned to their hotel room across from the Capitol building. That evening, they were going to see more of the city's monuments, which looked like shimmering jewels when they were lit at night. The monuments honored past presidents and soldiers who fought to keep the United States free. But now, it was time to rest.

Roberto got out his diary and wrote.

Today was one of the best days I've ever had. I saw the airplane that Wilbur Wright flew over Kitty Hawk. I also saw Glamorous Glennis, the X-1 rocket plane that Chuck Yeager flew when he broke the sound barrier. The Mercury space capsule that Scott Carpenter used to orbit Earth was barely taller than my dad!

When I was in the simulator, I really felt like I was a pilot. Sometimes, I had to close my eyes as we zoomed around. I took off and landed the airplane with only a little help from the cadet. I definitely want to be an Air Force pilot!

Name _____

Read the story on page 8. Then, answer the questions.

1. Where is Roberto originally from?

   _____

2. Although Roberto does not actually learn to fly in the story, the author chose "Learning to Fly" as the title. Why?

   _____

   _____

   _____

3. Choose one of the words in bold print. What does it mean? How do you know?

   _____

   _____

4. Underline the simile in the story. What is being compared?

   _____

   _____

5. The author states that Roberto is overwhelmed when they arrive at the National Air and Space Museum. What caused Roberto to feel this way?

   _____

   _____

   _____

Reflect

The author concludes the story with a first-person diary excerpt. How does this help deepen the reader's understanding of the story?

_____

_____

_____

_____

_____

Name _____

Read. Then, answer the questions.

Javon's Bike

Every kid on Javon's block had a bike. Javon wanted one too. He watched his friends ride off to the park. They waved and asked him to join them. He waved back. It was three blocks to the park. Walking was so slow that by time he got there, it would be time to go home.

One night, Javon asked his mother for a bike for his birthday. His mother explained that they did not have enough money. Javon went to his room. How would he ever get a bike? Just then, he remembered his teacher saying, "Where there's a will, there's a way."

The next day, Javon saw Mrs. Benson pulling weeds. She was an older woman, so he asked if she needed help. She said yes and sent him to the shed to get gloves. When Javon opened the shed door, he saw a bike. It was old and the tires were flat, but it looked beautiful to him.

Mrs. Benson told him that it belonged to her son and asked Javon if he liked it. She told him that when they finished she would give him a cool glass of lemonade—and the bike. How could he have dreamed that Mrs. Benson would give him such a fine gift for such a little favor?

1. What is Javon's problem? How does he solve it?

_____

2. Javon's teacher tells him, "Where there's a will, there's a way." What does she mean by this?

_____

_____

3. Compare and contrast how Javon sees the bike to how it actually looks.

_____

_____

 **Reflect**

What lesson does Javon learn in the story? What events in the story support the lesson?

_____

_____

_____

_____

Read. Then, answer the questions.

Jessica's New Room

School was going to begin, and Jessica had mixed feelings about the fourth grade. Her older sister had spent the summer warning Jessica about the dangers of fourth grade.

One day, Jessica got an idea. She needed a fourth-grader's bedroom. Jessica's room had many reminders of her early school years. She needed a more grown-up-looking room. She gathered some magazines with decorating tips and walked to her mother's basement office. She knew her mother liked well-thought-out ideas and presentations, so she prepared her thoughts on the way.

She found her mother and explained that she was very excited about being a top-notch fourth grader. Then, she went on to say that for this to happen, she needed a change.

Jessica placed several magazines on the table and explained that she was no longer a baby. She showed some pictures of older-looking bedroom styles, and her mother looked at each one carefully.

Her mother smiled and told her that it was a great idea. For almost an hour, Jessica and her mother swapped ideas and planned her new room.

Jessica was excited about the change from her old room and was certain this would help make her year in the fourth grade a good one.

1. How long does it take Jessica and her mother to plan her new room?

_____

2. The author states that Jessica has "mixed feelings" about going into fourth grade. How do you know?

_____

_____

3. How do Jessica's actions help support the theme?

_____

_____

 **Reflect**

How do Jessica's feelings change from the beginning of the story to the end? Use evidence from the story to support your answer.

_____

_____

Name _____

Read. Then, answer the questions on page 13.

The Mysterious Light

Chris sat in a chair by the window. The grandfather clock at the bottom of the stairs started to chime. It echoed through the quiet halls.

Chris could hardly keep his eyes open. He knew that his pajamas were laid neatly on the bed, but he did not want to wear them. If he had to run for help, he wanted to be wearing a shirt, jeans, and sneakers.

When his parents said that he could stay with his uncle while they were in France, he was happy. His other choice was Camp Blue Sky. Chris did not like Camp Blue Sky. At least at his uncle's house, he would have good food, a room of his own, and no leather crafts.

He closed his eyes and counted the clock's strikes—9, 10, 11, 12. He now wished that he had chosen Camp Blue Sky. It was not perfect, but it was better than a spooky, old house.

The clock stopped chiming. The house was still. Chris opened his eyes and looked down on the garden. He wanted to see the mysterious light again. If he knew what it was, he might be able to sleep.

At first, he saw nothing but dark paths and the reflection of the half moon on the pond. Maybe the light that he saw the night before was just a dream.

Suddenly, he saw it again. At first, the white beam **flickered**. Then, it was steady. It moved across the far side of the garden just beyond the garage. When it came toward the house, Chris dove into bed.

He pulled the covers over his head and waited. His heart pounded. His bedroom door slowly creaked open. He tried to stay still, but he could not help shaking when a voice spoke his name.

"Chris, are you still awake?"

Chris was startled to hear his name called. He sat up in bed and said, "Uncle Jeff, is that you?"

"Yes. I was outside checking on the cat in the barn. Koko just had her kittens. Would you like to come see them?"

"Sure!" said Chris. He jumped out of bed and reached for his shoes.

His uncle looked puzzled. "Chris," he said. "Why are you wearing your clothes in bed?"

Chris laughed. "It's a long story, Uncle Jeff. I'll tell you on the way to the barn."

Name _____

Read the story on page 12. Then, answer the questions.

1. What does *flickered* mean? How do you know?

_____

_____

2. Is this story told in first- or third-person narration? Circle the evidence in the story that supports your answer.

_____

_____

3. Why is the title a good choice for the story?

_____

_____

4. What is the mysterious light? How do you know?

_____

_____

_____

Reflect

Why does Chris suddenly go from being scared to laughing? What causes this change?

_____

_____

_____

_____

_____

_____

_____

_____

_____

Name _____

Read. Then, answer the questions.

Uri's Music

Uri loved to listen to music. As soon as he came home from school, his mother let him listen while he did homework.

Uri's father was a judge and worked long hours. Uri's music bothered his father, so he told Uri that he could not listen to music after six o'clock. This was bad news for Uri, but he turned off the music.

Uri missed his rock music so he asked his father if he could listen with headphones. His father agreed. He did his homework and chores with the headphones on. This worked out well for everyone.

One day, Uri's father asked him a question, but Uri did not hear it because he was wearing his headphones. His father grew angry and told Uri that he could not listen to music while he did his homework. This was bad news for Uri, but he turned off the music.

Uri continued to listen to music while he did chores. One day, as he reached to put away clean dishes, the cord got caught on the drawer. It jerked across Uri's arms and he dropped the dishes that he was holding. They broke all over the floor. His parents came running, and when they learned what had happened, they took the player away. Uri finished the dishes in silence.

Uri missed his music and **proposed** to his parents that he be allowed to listen in his room until dinnertime. After dinner, they would turn on classical music. Uri's parents knew that music was important to Uri, so they agreed.

1. What does *proposed* mean? How do you know?

_____

2. What would be a better title for this story? Why?

_____

_____

3. How would the story be different if it were told from Uri's father's point of view?

_____

_____

 Reflect

Uri has a few problems in the story. Do you think he is a good problem solver? Why or why not? Use evidence from the story to support your answer.

_____

_____

Read. Then, answer the questions.

Alone

Derrick came straight home from school today. He was eager to play his new computer game. Derrick turned the knob of the front door. It was locked!

Derrick's mom was always home before him. She left work each day at three o'clock. It was 3:45, and she still was not home.

Derrick was worried, but he decided to try to get into the house. He tried the side door. It was locked. The back door was locked too. He thought about climbing in through a window.

Derrick felt his throat tighten, and tears came to his eyes. He decided he would not cry, and he wiped his eyes. "Think," he said to himself.

Just then, Derrick's neighbor Mrs. Phillips drove up her driveway. He ran right over and told her his mom was not home and he was locked out. She told him to call his mom and wait there for her. He sat at the kitchen counter.

Derrick called the bookstore where his mom worked. Her boss said that she had left on time. He felt his stomach tighten again and wondered what could have happened. Derrick started to dial his grandma's phone number. At that moment, he saw his mom's car pull up in the driveway. He thanked Mrs. Phillips and ran out the door.

Derrick ran to his mom. She stepped out of the car and into his hug. "I'm so sorry," she said. "I was stuck in traffic on the highway. There was an accident. I didn't move for twenty minutes. All I could think about was you waiting for me. Are you OK?"

Derrick told his mom what he had done. He said, "I wasn't worried for a minute!"

1. Why does Derrick go straight home from school?

_____

2. What causes Derrick's mom to be late?

_____

3. The story is about a boy who is worried about his mom. What evidence does the author provide to support this?

_____

_____

 **Reflect**

How would the story be different if it were told from Derrick's mother's point of view?

_____

_____

Read the stories on pages 15 and 16. Then, answer the questions.

Erika's Secret

Erika and Samaria were excited because they were going to the beach. Erika had never been before.

Samaria told Erika all about the paddleboat. "I like to paddle to the deep part and jump into the water," said Samaria. Erika felt her stomach tighten. She did not know how to swim. She did not know that Samaria was so brave.

At the beach, the girls played in the water, jumping in the waves and laughing. Erika thought the beach was great!

Then, Samaria's dad called them over to the boat dock. He had the paddleboat ready for them and held two life jackets in his hands. Erika was very nervous. Samaria's dad helped her put on her life jacket. Erika put her feet on the pedals. Samaria started pedaling, so Erika did too. Soon they were moving quickly across the water. It was fun. When they were far out in the ocean, Samaria stopped the boat and jumped in the water. Erika did not move. She did not dare tell Samaria that she could not swim. Would Samaria laugh at her?

Samaria watched Erika and guessed what was wrong. She climbed back into the boat. "Do you know how to swim yet?" she asked kindly. Erika shook her head. Samaria smiled at her friend and said, "Let's paddle around some more. Then, after lunch, I'll teach you a little bit about swimming." Erika smiled at her best friend. Why had she ever worried about telling Samaria that she did not know how to swim?

1. What causes Erika's stomach to tighten?

_____

2. Describe all of Erika's emotions and provide the causes for each.

_____

_____

3. Describe Erika and Samaria's friendship.

_____

_____

⚙ Reflect

Look back at the story "Alone" on page 15. Compare and contrast the stories. Be sure to include the theme and traits of the main characters in your comparison.

_____

_____

_____

Name _____

Read. Then, answer the questions on page 18.

A Family Hike

We started hiking on the trail early in the morning. The sun was rising in the sky, and the air around us was cold and misty. The pine trees looked like arrows pointing our way to the top of the mountain. It was a wonderful morning.

My mom and dad each carried a heavy backpack full of food, tents, water, and other things. Ben and I carried packs too. Mine only had my clothes and a sleeping bag in it. I carried a few snacks in my pockets and two water bottles on my belt. Ben is bigger than I am, so he carried some food and a cookstove in his pack.

We walked quietly at first. My dad always says that **you do not need words to be part of the forest in the morning**. I could hear birds singing and chipmunks moving through the leaves on the ground. There was no breeze, so the trees were silent. We walked single file along the trail.

At lunchtime, we stopped by a stream that flowed down the mountain. We could see a small waterfall higher up, but here, the water cut through the rock and snaked past flowers and bushes. We took off our shoes and dipped our feet in the water. The sun shone brightly overhead, and we all took off our jackets.

I knew better than to ask how much farther we had to go. My parents always say that **our destination is the hike itself**. We would be walking for three days on these trails. We would see many beautiful sights and hear and smell things we do not hear or smell at home in the city. My mom and dad are teachers. Every summer, we take a trip as a family. Ben wanted to bring a teenage friend, but my dad said that this was family time. Ben complained, but I know he likes family trips too.

At dinnertime, we stopped and set up our tents on a flat meadow. We could see the next mountain peak from our site. It looked beautiful as the sun set behind it. We lit a fire and cooked dinner. We stayed awake a while longer to watch the stars. My mom pointed out several constellations. I want to be an astronomer someday.

We went to bed pretty early because we were all tired from walking. Tomorrow, we will have another long walk. We will reach the top of the mountain tomorrow. I have never stood on a mountaintop before. My dad always says that **I will be able to see forever**. I think I will like that. Maybe, I will be able to see my friend Gena's house back home. I will wave to her and shout hello. I will hear the echo and pretend that she shouted back at me. But that is tomorrow, and my dad always says that **even the night is part of the journey**. So, I will close my eyes and listen for the owls, the wind in the trees, and the sound of my dad snoring. I love this place!

Name _____

Read the story on page 17. Then, answer the questions.

1. How many days will the family be hiking?

_____

2. Is the story told in first- or third-person narration? Circle evidence in the story that supports your answer.

_____

_____

3. The author uses many descriptive words and phrases in the story. Underline at least five. How do they affect the reader?

_____

_____

4. The author states that "the trees were silent." What does this mean? What evidence helped you understand?

_____

_____

5. What details in the story support the idea that the family enjoys time together?

_____

_____

_____

 Reflect

Read the bold phrases. What do they tell the reader about the parents? What lesson do the parents want the narrator to understand?

_____

_____

_____

_____

_____

_____

_____

Name _____

Read. Then, answer the questions.

A New Outlook

Penny had a hard time seeing the board in class. Rosa sat next to her. Penny asked Rosa to read her the assignment each day. One day, their teacher said, "Penny, I think you should go to the eye doctor."

Penny's mom made an appointment with an **optometrist**. At the appointment, Penny went into a darkened room, and the doctor pulled a machine over to her. He told Penny to look through the mask and read some letters on the opposite wall. The doctor kept turning dials until Penny said that the letters were very clear and easy to read.

After this, an optician helped her choose frames for her new glasses. Penny chose small, round frames that were black. The optician told Penny that her glasses would be ready in about a week.

In a week, Penny and her mom went back to pick up her new glasses. She liked the way she looked with her glasses. Her mom said she looked smart.

The next day at school, Penny wore her new glasses. She could not wait to show her friends. Rosa smiled, but Penny was surprised to hear someone call her "four eyes."

During math, Penny could see the problems on the board. She had no trouble reading her book. She felt great about how clear everything was now. The next time she heard someone say "four eyes," Penny said, "The better to see you with, my dear." Penny and her friends laughed so hard, they almost cried.

1. What is an *optometrist*? How do you know?

_____

2. List at least four ways that having glasses helps Penny.

_____

_____

3. Describe Penny and Rosa's friendship. Use evidence from the story to support your answer.

_____

_____

 **Reflect**

At the end of the story, Penny makes a joke when someone calls her "four eyes." Why does she do this?

_____

_____

Name _____

Read. Then, answer the questions on page 21.

Sailing in a Storm

Tina and her dad loved to go sailing together. One summer, they decided to sail to Beaver Island. They put the boat into the water in Charlevoix, Michigan, around six o'clock on a Thursday night. They planned to dock the boat, shop and eat in town, and then set out for the island in the morning. Unfortunately, the marina did not have any available docks for their boat. They had no other choice but to motor across the lake to the island that night.

Tina's dad motored the 23-foot sailboat through the channel and out into Lake Michigan. It was a quiet evening. The sky was clear, and there was no wind. He put up the sails, but they just flopped lightly in the calm air. The motor pushed them across the wide water. They listened to music and ate cheese and avocado sandwiches.

Around ten o'clock, a **brisk** wind picked up suddenly. They turned off the motor and sailed with the wind. Very quickly, the wind grew too strong and the waves became large. The small boat leaned and moved quickly through the water as the wind filled the sails.

When water started splashing into the boat, Tina's dad shouted, "We have to take down the sails! I can't handle this much wind!" Tina was scared. Her dad wanted her to go up on deck and take down the sails. She was afraid that a wave might wash her overboard or that she might lose her balance. She decided to stay back and steer the boat instead. But Tina didn't like that either. It was hard to control the boat in the strong wind.

Tina's dad went up on deck to take down the sails. Tina was shivering. The cold water soaked her each time the boat crashed through a wave. But, she was shaking more from fear than cold. What would she do if her dad fell into the water? She did not think she could turn the boat around to get him. She wondered if they would ever make it to the island.

Once Tina's dad had tied up the sails, he took over the steering. Soon, the waves grew smaller, the wind died down, and several stars appeared in the sky as the clouds moved away. They motored ahead in silence.

When the island came into sight, Tina sat on the bow of the boat and watched. She thought nothing had ever looked so beautiful as the island with its sheltered bay. They anchored the boat in the bay and put up a mooring light. They unrolled their sleeping bags inside the cabin and went quickly to sleep.

Name _____

Read the story on page 20. Then, answer the questions.

1. What does *brisk* mean? How do you know?

_____

_____

2. The author uses many descriptive words and phrases in the story. Underline at least five.

3. What makes the boat so hard to control?

_____

4. Describe Tina. Use evidence from the story to support your answer.

_____

_____

5. What is the central message of the story?

_____

_____

6. Which details in the story support the central message?

_____

_____

_____

Reflect

After the storm, Tina and her father "motored ahead in silence." Why do you think that they were quiet?

_____

_____

_____

_____

_____

_____

_____

Name _____

Read. Then, answer the questions.

The Fort

All of the kids in the neighborhood loved to play in the fort, a small fenced-in area behind an empty house. The house had been empty for six months. Every day, the kids played in the fort. One day, someone bought the house. The kids all wondered what would happen to the fort.

A new family with little kids moved into the house. That was promising. Who would ask them about using the fort? The neighborhood kids played in the front yards together, but all they talked about was the fort.

When the kids went back to school, they talked about the fort again. "We should ask the new neighbors if we can play there," said Alex. The kids agreed and sent Alex and Brian to knock on the door. When the door opened, Alex nervously asked, "May we play in the fort behind your house? We will be careful."

"I don't know," said the new owner, Mrs. Johnson. "Let's go back there, and you can show me what you are going to do there. Then, we can talk about it."

The kids showed her how they got in and where they played. Mrs. Johnson said, "OK. You may play here if you promise to play safely and pretty quietly."

That sounded fair to everyone. Now, they meet at the fort after school. Once in a while, they have little visitors from the Johnson house. The kids come in and have tea parties. Mrs. Johnson supplies the tea and cookies.

1. Why do the kids have to stop playing in the fort?

_____

2. What is the main idea of the story?

_____

_____

3. Underline the details in the story that support the main idea.

Reflect

In the story, the kids solve their problem by talking to the new owners of the house. What is another solution the author could have used? How might the story have ended if the kids had chosen that solution?

_____

_____

_____

_____

Name _____

Read. Then, answer the questions.

The Lemonade Stand

Daysha and Emily set up a small table at the corner of Cambridge and Sherman Streets. Daysha set up the supplies, and Emily set up two chairs and an umbrella. Soon, they would be open for business.

The girls painted a sign that said "Lemonade for Sale." They leaned the sign in front of the table.

Then, they went inside and came back with a cooler that had two pitchers of lemonade and a bag of ice. They also had a container of homemade cookies.

They took one pitcher and set it on the table. Then, they placed 10 cookies on a plate. They sat in their chairs and waited.

A car drove by but did not stop. Another car drove past. Emily yelled, "Lemonade for sale! Twenty-five cents a cup!" The car kept driving. A third car came by and parked at the neighbor's house. Daysha and Emily both made a **ruckus**. "Lemonade for sale! Twenty-five cents a cup!" The neighbor waved at the girls and walked over to the lemonade stand. She gave the girls a quarter and bought lemonade and two cookies before saying good-bye.

Emily and Daysha stayed at their stand for two hours. Many people bought lemonade and cookies. By the time the girls ran out, they had earned six dollars.

1. How much do the girls charge for the lemonade?

_____

2. Is the story told in first- or third-person narration? Circle the evidence in the story that supports your answer.

_____

3. The girls make a *ruckus*. Why?

_____

_____

Reflect

What is the setting of the story? Why is this important to the outcome?

_____

_____

_____

_____

Read. Then, answer the questions.

The Shortcut

We probably should have taken the road home from the baseball park. It was getting dark, though, and we decided to take the shortcut home. I was the oldest and should have made a better choice. I did not know there would be a train.

The shortcut from the baseball park to home was along the train tracks. After Reggie's game was over, we were excited. The game had gone into overtime, and Reggie's team had won! Samantha and little Brittany were running to keep up while they chewed on their candy necklaces. When we came to the turn for the shortcut, we were so excited and happy that we just took it. We should have stayed on the road.

We walked for about five minutes on the tracks. The sides were steep, and there were thick bushes and marshy water at the bottom. We stayed on the tracks. Samantha asked how we would know if a train was coming. I said that we would feel the tracks rumbling.

It was then that I heard the train whistle far away. You never can tell when a train will come through. I did not want to worry the little ones, so I said calmly, "Let's go back to the road." We turned around, and I walked pretty fast. Everyone followed.

Soon, we felt the tracks rumbling, and I shouted, "Run!" I grabbed little Brittany in my arms, and Reggie held Samantha's hand. We ran as fast as we could. Then I could see the headlights, and the train blew its loud whistle. We kept running, and I shouted, "Get off the tracks, NOW!" We jumped off the tracks. We all slid down the sides, trying hard to keep out of the scratchy bushes. Samantha and Brittany were crying, but I could not hear them. The loud train was rushing by us.

After the train went by, we climbed back up the hill. We were all scratched up from the bushes, but no one complained. We were all shaking as we walked back to the road. We did not have to talk. We knew we would never take the shortcut home again.

1. Why are the kids excited at the beginning of the story?

_____

2. How would the narrator know if a train was coming?

_____

3. What causes the narrator to turn around and begin walking back to the road?

_____

☀ Reflect

Describe how the train impacts the mood of the story.

_____

_____

_____

Name _____

Read. Then, answer the questions on page 26.

Henry Wadsworth Longfellow was a nineteenth-century American poet. Back then, most villages and towns had blacksmiths who shaped metal. Longfellow wrote this poem about an honest and hard-working blacksmith.

The Village Blacksmith

Under a spreading chestnut tree
The village smithy stands;
The smith, a mighty man is he,
With large and sinewy hands;
And the muscles of his **brawny arms**
Are strong as iron bands.

His hair is crisp, and black, and long,
His face is like the tan;
His brow is wet with honest sweat,
He earns what'er he can,
And looks the whole world in the face,
For he owes not any man.

Week in, week out, from morn till night,
You can hear his bellows blow;
You can hear him swing his heavy sledge,
With measured beat and slow,
Like a sexton ringing the village bell,
When the evening sun is low.

And children coming home from school
Look in at the open door;
They love to see the flaming forge,
And hear the bellows roar,
And catch the burning sparks that fly
Like chaff from a threshing floor.

He goes on Sunday to the church,
And sits among his boys;
He hears the parson pray and preach,
He hears his daughter's voice,
Singing in the village choir,
And it makes his heart rejoice.

It sounds to him like her mother's voice,
Singing in Paradise!
He needs must think of her once more,
How in the grave she lies;
And with his hard, rough hand he wipes
A tear out of his eyes.

Toiling,—rejoicing,—sorrowing
Onward through life he goes;
Each morning sees some task begin,
Each evening sees it close;
Something attempted, something done,
Has earned a night's repose.

Thanks, thanks to thee, my worthy friend,
For the lesson thou hast taught!
Thus at the flaming forge of life
Our fortunes must be wrought;
Thus on its sounding anvil shaped
Each burning deed and thought.

Name _____

Read the text on page 25. Then, answer the questions.

1. What type of text is it?

_____

2. Label all of the structural elements.

3. In stanza one, the author describes the blacksmith's "brawny arms." What does this mean? How do you know?

_____

_____

4. What makes the blacksmith's heart rejoice?

_____

_____

_____

5. Longfellow wants the reader to see the man as more than just a blacksmith. Circle the stanzas that support this. What did Longfellow want the reader to understand?

_____

_____

Reflect

Before the poem, it is stated that the blacksmith is "honest and hard-working." How does the author support this description in the poem?

_____

_____

_____

_____

_____

_____

_____

_____

_____

Name _____

Read. Then, answer the questions on page 28.

Robert Louis Stevenson wrote the timeless adventure books *Kidnapped* (Stevenson Books, 2013) and *Treasure Island* (CreateSpace, 2013). Published in 1885, Stevenson's collection of poems, *A Child's Garden of Verses*, contains some of the best-known nighttime poetry written.

The Land of Nod

From breakfast on through all the day
At home among my friends I stay;
But every night I go abroad
Afar into the Land of Nod.

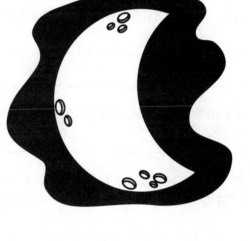

All by myself I have to go,
With none to tell me what to do—
All alone beside the streams
And up the mountain-sides of dreams.

The strangest things are there for me,
Both things to eat and things to see,
And many frightening sights abroad
Till morning in the Land of Nod.

Try as I like to find the way,
I never can get back by day,
Nor can remember plain and clear
The curious music that I hear.

Shadow March (from "North-West Passage")

All round the house is the jet-black night;
It stares through the window-pane;
It crawls in the corners, hiding from the light
And it moves with the moving flame.

Now my little heart goes a-beating like a drum,
With the breath of the Bogie in my hair,
And all round the candle the crooked shadows come,
And go marching along up the stair.

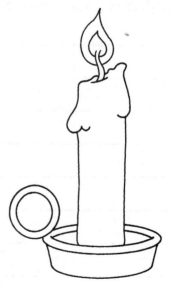

The shadows of the balusters, the shadow of the lamp,
The shadow of the child that goes to bed—
All the wicked shadows coming tramp, tramp, tramp,
With the black night overhead.

Name _____

Read the text on page 27. Then, answer the questions.

1. In both poems, circle the adjectives the author uses to paint a picture in the mind of the reader.

2. What is the main idea of "The Land of Nod"? Underline the evidence in the poem that supports the main idea.

   _____

   _____

3. How does the author of "Shadow March" feel about nighttime? Use evidence from the story to support your answer.

   _____

   _____

4. Underline the simile in "Shadow March." What two things are being compared?

   _____

5. In "Shadow March," Stevenson writes, "All the wicked shadows coming, tramp, tramp, tramp." Why did he choose to repeat the word *tramp*?

   _____

   _____

 Reflect

Compare and contrast the two poems. Be sure to address the theme of each poem, as well as the author's point of view.

_____

_____

_____

_____

_____

_____

_____

_____

_____

Read. Then, answer the questions.

Marc Brown

Marc Brown is the best-selling author of the Arthur books. They tell about the life of an aardvark, his family, and his quirky animal friends.

Marc Brown loves drawing and telling stories. His Grandma Thora told wonderful stories. Mr. Brown got his love of telling stories from her. One day, he told a story about an aardvark named Arthur. That was how the Arthur stories were born.

His wonderful Grandma Thora loved his drawings. She saved them and told him to draw more. She did not usually save things. Marc Brown draws the pictures for all of the Arthur books and writes the stories.

The first Arthur book was published in 1976. That book was called *Arthur's Nose*. In the more recent books, Arthur's nose has gotten smaller so that he could show more expressions on Arthur's face. Marc Brown has written at least 30 other Arthur books.

The ideas for the Arthur stories come from Mr. Brown's experiences. They also come from when his own boys were young and from life with his young daughter, Eliza. In many of Marc Brown's books, you can find the names of his sons, Tolon and Tucker. He writes their names on packages in stores, on jackets, and in other small places.

1. What is the title of the first Arthur book?

_____

2. How does the author support the idea that Marc Brown's Grandma Thora loved his drawings?

_____

_____

3. The author of the text uses a descriptive text structure. What key ideas about Marc Brown is the author describing?

_____

_____

 Reflect

The author ends the article by stating, "In many of Marc Brown's books, you can find the names of his sons, Tolon and Tucker." Why?

_____

_____

_____

Name _____

Read. Then, answer the questions.

Water Clocks

The **clepsydra** (klep-sa-dra), or water clock, is an inventive clock for cloudy days or indoor use. It had its origins in Egypt. Clepsydra is a Greek word that means "water thief." Some clocks could be used only once. The clepsydras could be used repeatedly.

People have built water clocks for more than three millennia. Although the clocks are different, one basic rule remained the same. Water constantly dripped through a small hole in one container's bottom and into another container.

Egyptian clock makers formed clay pots with tiny holes in the bottoms and carved lines around the sides. As water slowly dripped out of one pot and into another, it was possible to tell how much time had passed by the changing water level.

In museums, you can see ancient clepsydras that are glazed in beautiful colors with designs from the night sky. Some clepsydras had brass bells that rang or wooden doors that opened to reveal tiny dancing people.

Although sunlight was not needed for a clepsydra to work, the temperature caused several problems. When it became very cold, the water froze and did not drip. When it was very hot, the water evaporated quickly. Eventually, the dripping sound of the clepsydra was replaced by the ticktock of the mechanical clock. The first mechanical clock was built in the late fourteenth century.

1. What is a *clepsydra*?

_____

2. What is the effect of cold weather on the clepsydra?

_____

_____

3. Why does the author state that the clepsydra is an inventive clock?

_____

_____

 **Reflect**

Based on the information in the text, what could have led to the invention of mechanical clocks?

_____

_____

_____

_____

Read. Then, answer the questions.

Where Is Amelia?

Amelia Earhart flew airplanes at a time when women rarely did such things. She made many daring trips and was the first woman to fly solo across the Atlantic Ocean. In 1937, Amelia planned to fly around the world. Instead, she **vanished**.

She and her copilot made it to the Pacific Ocean. On July 2, 1937, they planned to fly to a tiny island. However, many things went wrong. The day was supposed to be clear, but it was not. The flight took longer than planned. Amelia sent a message to say that her airplane was getting low on gas. In her last static-filled message, she said that she could not see the island. She was never heard from again.

The president of the United States called for a search. It lasted two weeks. No clues were ever found.

At first, people thought that the airplane had just run out of gas. It must have crashed into the sea and sunk too low to be found. Other people said that Earhart was looking for facts about Japanese ships. Was Amelia Earhart a spy?

The search goes on for Amelia Earhart. One person thought that he had found her grave. Other people have found parts of airplanes. They thought the parts were from the crash of Earhart's airplane. But, many airplanes crashed into the Pacific Ocean during World War II.

No proof has ever been found that Amelia Earhart was a spy. Her body and her airplane have never been found. We may never know the whole story about this great pilot. She is gone, but her story lives on.

1. When did Amelia Earhart disappear?

_____

2. The author chose "Where Is Amelia?" as the title. What details in the story support this choice?

_____

3. What does *vanished* mean? Underline the text that supports your answer.

_____

☀ Reflect

Choose two words that you would use to describe Amelia Earhart. Use evidence from the story to support your answer.

_____

_____

_____

Name _____

Read. Then, answer the questions on page 33.

Whales

There are many different kinds of whales. Whales are not fish; they are mammals. They swim in the water, but they breathe air. Whales breathe through the blowholes on the top of their heads. They have smooth skin that allows them to move quickly in the water. Whales use their strong tails to push themselves forward. They have a thick layer of blubber under their skin that keeps them warm. There are two main groups of whales: toothed whales and baleen whales.

Toothed whales have teeth and eat fish, squid, and other sea animals. Baleen whales do not have teeth. Instead, they have baleens that they use to strain their food.

Blue whales are one type of baleen whale. Blue whales are not only the largest whales, but they are also the largest animals that have ever lived. A blue whale can grow to be nearly 100 feet (30 m) long. The blue whale's tongue alone can weigh as much as an elephant.

Blue whales like to eat krill, which are tiny shrimp. Krill live in cold water, so blue whales spend their summers near the North and South Poles. They spend their winters in warmer water where there is less krill. When there is not much krill, the whales need to live off the blubber they have stored in their bodies.

Sperm whales are one type of toothed whale. Sperm whales may grow to be 70 feet (20 m) long. Sperm whales have the largest brains of any animal. Their brains are about the size of a basketball and weigh more than 15 pounds (7 kg).

Sperm whales are strong and powerful and like to eat squid. Squid are tough animals. The whales need to fight the squid in order to eat them. Sperm whales live all over the world, but they usually stay away from the coldest waters near the North and South Poles. Sperm whales have large heads that are filled with a waxy substance called spermaceti. The spermaceti may help the whale float.

For hundreds of years, people have hunted whales for their meat and blubber. Hunters have sold the parts of the whale for money. The blue whale's baleen was once sold to make jewelry. The sperm whale's spermaceti was sold to make candles and makeup. Some whales were becoming endangered because of the hunting. Now, whale hunting is against the law in most countries.

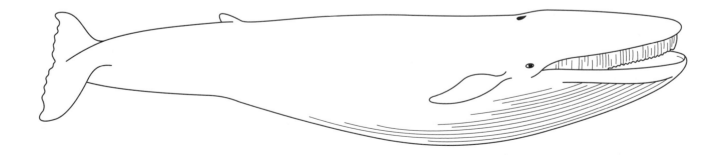

Name _____

Read the passage on page 32. Then, answer the questions.

1. What do blue whales like to eat?

   _____

2. What is the effect of people hunting whales?

   _____

   _____

3. What text structure does the author use to organize the passage? How do you know?

   _____

   _____

   _____

4. How does the author support the fact that blue whales and sperm whales both need blubber to survive?

   _____

   _____

   _____

☀ Reflect

Why does the author switch focus in the last paragraph? What does the author want the reader to understand?

_____

_____

_____

_____

_____

_____

_____

_____

Name _____

Read. Then, answer the questions on page 35.

Day Poetry

Robert Louis Stevenson was born on November 13, 1850, in Edinburgh, Scotland. He grew up in a wealthy family and received an excellent education from private tutors. His father was an engineer who designed magnificent lighthouses along the rocky coastline of Scotland. Stevenson knew that his father wanted him to become an engineer too. But, Robert had a different idea.

By the time Stevenson was 17 years old, he decided to become a writer. Reading about traveling had recently become popular in Europe. Luckily for him, he liked to travel. By writing for travel magazines, Stevenson was able to have the best of what he loved. He could write and get paid by a publisher to travel to wonderful places.

At first, Stevenson wrote for adults. Then, in 1881, he was on vacation along the shores of Scotland with his family. They had the misfortune of rainy weather the entire vacation. While cooped up in a house with teenagers, he began to write *Treasure Island* (Frederick Singer & Sons, August 2013). When the book was published and sold out at stores all over Great Britain, Stevenson knew that he should write for children. He also wrote a book of poetry called *A Child's Garden of Verses* (Chronicle Books, March 2004). Stevenson spent years traveling through Europe and as far away as California. His travels made him aware of time and the objects in the sky. These are subjects of many of his stories and poems.

The Sun's Travels

The sun is not a-bed, when I
At night upon my pillow lie;
Still round the earth his way he takes,
And morning after morning makes.

While here at home, in shining day,
We round the sunny garden play,
Each little Indian sleepy-head
Is being kissed and put to bed.

And when at eve I rise from tea,
Day dawns beyond the Atlantic Sea;
And all the children in the West
Are getting up and being dressed.

Time to Rise

A birdie with a yellow bill
Hopped upon the window sill,
Cocked his shining eye and said:
"Ain't you 'shamed, you
        sleepy-head!"

Read the text on page 34. Then, answer the questions.

1. What did Robert Louis Stevenson's father want him to be?

_____

2. What was the effect of the rainy weather during Stevenson's vacation?

_____

_____

3. The author writes the article using a chronological text structure. Underline the evidence in the text that supports this.

4. How did Stevenson know that he should write for children?

_____

_____

5. The author includes two poems at the end of the text. How does this help the reader's understanding of the text?

_____

_____

_____

 **Reflect**

Why does the author specifically choose these two poems to include? Use evidence from both the passage and the poems to support your answer.

_____

_____

_____

_____

_____

_____

_____

_____

Read. Then, answer the questions.

Insects

Insects are amazing animals. They come in beautiful colors and a variety of shapes. They live in cold and hot climates and in wet jungles and dry deserts. They can live underground and high in the trees. There are at least one million different species of insects, and every year, new species are discovered.

Insects do many of the same things we do but in unique ways. Some insects hear with hairs that cover their bodies. Other insects have hearing organs on their legs. Some insects hear from the sides of their bodies.

Some insects are beneficial to people. Bees make honey. Bees, wasps, butterflies, and other insects pollinate plants. Some insects eat or destroy pests that ruin our crops. Some people even eat insects!

Some insects are harmful to people. Some insects eat our crops. Some insects get into homes and destroy clothes, books, and stored foods. Termites chew the wood frames of buildings. Worst of all, some insects carry diseases that can make people sick or die.

Although all insects have six legs, three body parts, and two antennae, each species of insects looks and acts uniquely. Insects can be beautiful or ugly, helpful or harmful, or noisy or quiet. Insects help make the world a very interesting place.

1. How many different species of insects are there?

_____

2. What are three unique ways that insects hear?

_____

_____

3. The author states that "insects are amazing animals." What evidence in the text supports this statement?

_____

_____

 Reflect

The author writes about insects being both beneficial and harmful to people. Choose one of these statements to defend. Use evidence from the text to support your opinion.

_____

_____

_____

Name _____

Read. Then, answer the questions on page 38.

President Says No to World Calendar

by Samantha Warts

The Zipper Press

NEW YORK CITY – The United Nations met yesterday to discuss the idea of a World Calendar. US President Dwight D. Eisenhower's close friend, Henry Cabot Lodge, told the gathering of nations that the United States was against the plan.

> The United Nations is a large "club" of countries. Its goals include improving peace among nations, providing disaster relief, protecting human rights, and fostering social and economic development.

Lodge explained that President Eisenhower felt that the World Calendar would be unfair to people of Jewish or Muslim faiths. These religions use a calendar based on the orbit of the moon around Earth. The World Calendar, however, is based on the orbit of Earth around the sun.

Elisabeth Achelis designed the World Calendar 25 years ago. Her calendar is broken into exactly 52 weeks. Each year would have 364 days instead of the 365 days we have now.

Achelis insists that the present calendar, which Pope Gregory XIII created in 1582, is wrong. In a recent interview with the *New England Post*, she said, "The calendar we use today is more than 400 years old. From year to year, no one ever seems to know on what day of the week holidays, such as New Year's, will fall. It divides 365 days into seven-day weeks. The only problem is that you cannot do that! Pope Gregory's calendar has 365¼ days each year. I ask you, how do you have a fourth of a day?"

The World Calendar would have a day without a number following every December 30. This day, called Worldsday, would be a holiday throughout the world. Every four years, another day without a number would also follow June 30. It would be called Leap Year Day.

All holidays would fall on the same day every year. Christmas would always be on a Monday and New Year's on Sunday. If you were born on a Friday, your birthday would always be on a Friday.

President Eisenhower told reporters last week that the calendar idea bothered him. The president agreed that it would be easier for all nations to have identical timetables such as the World Calendar. Still, he believed that it would be unjust to religions that use a lunar calendar to set their holy days. President Eisenhower closed by saying, "I feel no change is needed. Our present calendar is perfectly fine."

Name _____

Read the article on page 37. Then, answer the questions.

1. Why did President Eisenhower disagree with the World Calendar?

_____

2. When was the present calendar created?

_____

3. What is Worldsday, and when would it occur?

_____

_____

_____

4. How does the sidebar help the reader better understand the article?

_____

_____

_____

5. What is the main idea of the article?

_____

_____

6. Underline the sentences in the article that support the main idea of the passage.

Reflect

Pretend that you believe in using the World Calendar. Use evidence from the article to support your opinion.

_____

_____

_____

_____

_____

_____

_____

_____

Name _____

Read. Then, answer the questions on page 40.

Managing Fires

Firefighters have a difficult but important job. They are highly trained and brave people who extinguish fires. They work hard to save people from getting hurt in fires and to prevent personal property from being damaged. But, there are some fires that firefighters do not try to extinguish.

In 1972, a new policy was written. It said that if a fire is started by lightning in a national forest or park, it should not be extinguished unless it causes a **threat** to buildings, personal property, or the logging industry. Now, firefighters must also decide if a fire should be left to burn or not.

Fire is a natural part of the life cycle of a forest. About every 300 years, a natural fire can clean up a mature forest that is overgrown with underbrush and crowded with fallen trees. The fire can burn the mess and make room for healthy new growth. These natural fires usually burn themselves out on their own.

When a natural fire occurs, firefighters carefully watch it burn. They make sure that the fire does not get out of control. A strong wind can make a natural fire grow too large and threaten areas where people work or live.

Some forest fires are not started naturally. A careless person might throw a burning cigarette and start a fire. Other careless campers may let a campfire get out of control. If one of these fires starts in the forest, the firefighters will immediately work to extinguish the fire.

When firefighters must extinguish a large fire in a forest, they use many different methods. Firefighters use water from local lakes and streams and hoses to try stop the flames. They may use axes to cut away trees that could burn and spread the fire. In some cases, they use bulldozers to push burnable materials away from the fire. Sometimes, airplanes drop chemicals over the fire. These chemicals slow down the fire. Another method is to light "backfires." A backfire is a small, controlled fire that burns the fuel (trees and shrubs) of a huge forest fire. Firefighters try to remove the materials that feed the fire so that the fire will stop.

All uncontrolled fires are dangerous. What a relief it is to know that we have brave, trained firefighters to keep fires under control!

Name _____

Read the passage on page 39. Then, answer the questions.

1. How did the new policy in 1972 change the job of a firefighter?

_____

_____

2. What does *threat* mean? How do you know?

_____

_____

3. Compare and contrast a firefighter's job as it relates to natural fires and fires that are started carelessly.

_____

_____

4. Explain the methods firefighters might use to extinguish a large forest fire.

_____

_____

_____

Reflect

Most of the passage discusses factual information about managing fires. Why does the author switch and include an opinion in the last paragraph?

_____

_____

_____

_____

_____

_____

_____

_____

_____

Name _____

Read. Then, answer the questions on page 42.

Yellowstone Fires

In 1988, Yellowstone National Park had a huge fire that burned nearly half of the park. Although this may sound like a terrible **tragedy**, the fires were actually a beneficial part of the forest's natural life cycle.

The fires in Yellowstone had to happen. For hundreds of years, the forests had been growing without any large fires. Over the years, many trees had grown and died. The tree trunks fell on the ground and stayed there. Eventually, the ground was covered with dead trees. This blocked the sun from new growth on the forest floor. It also made it difficult for animals to move around the forests. The park was becoming covered with forests. There were fewer meadows for new plants, and animals had less area for grazing.

Lightning started several fires in Yellowstone during the dry summer of 1988. The dead tree trunks on the forest floor ignited like firewood. The fires grew and grew. Firefighters worked hard to control the fires, but they could not stop them. They were able to protect some areas from burning, but the fires did not stop until some snow fell in September. Nature started the fires, and nature extinguished them in the end.

After the fires were out, the forests began to grow again. In some ways, the forests were better off after the fire. Some roots and seeds had remained safe underground during the fires. Others, such as lodgepole pine seeds, had been locked in cones that the heat from the fire released. The new plants that grew were not only beautiful, but they were also perfect food for the animals that had survived the fire. Most of the animals did survive the fire. Many of them prefer to live in the meadows that now cover much of the park. More than half of the 2.2-million-acre park was untouched by the fires, so plenty of forests still remain for the animals too.

Yellowstone National Park continues to grow and recover from the huge fires of 1988. As the park grows, new animals and plants find their homes there. In about 300 years, the park will be ready for a new fire to give it a fresh start once again.

Name _____

Read the passage on page 41. Then, answer the questions.

1. What does *tragedy* mean? How do you know?

_____

_____

2. What is the main idea of the passage?

_____

_____

3. How does the author support the idea that Yellowstone National Park was better as a result of the fire in 1988?

_____

_____

4. The author states that, "nature started the fires, and nature extinguished them in the end." What does the author mean? How does the author support this statement in the passage?

_____

_____

_____

_____

Reflect

Reread the last sentence of the passage. Do you agree? Use evidence from the text to support your answer.

_____

_____

_____

_____

_____

_____

_____

Name _____

Read the passages on pages 39 and 41. Then, answer the questions.

1. What important fact about natural forest fires is included in both passages?

_____

_____

2. Based on the information in both passages, how would the Yellowstone fires have been different if they had happened in 1960 instead of 1988?

_____

_____

_____

3. Both passages focus on fires. What makes the passages different from each other?

_____

_____

4. Write a different title for each selection. Why would each title work?

_____

_____

_____

Reflect

Reread the last sentence of "Yellowstone Fires." Would the author of "Managing Fires" agree? Why or why not?

_____

_____

_____

_____

_____

_____

_____

_____

Name _____

Read. Then, answer the questions.

Wolves

If you have read fairy tales, you may believe that all wolves are vicious, evil, and ruthless. They eat children, pigs, and other small animals. There is not anything good to say about wolves. Or, is there? Are wolves just misunderstood?

Wolves are actually nothing like the characters in fairy tales. While they do eat animals, wolves would never attack a child just for the sake of eating. They may attack people if the people threaten them. This happens rarely. Wolves tend to be shy animals.

Wolves are meat eaters, and they must hunt to get their food. They are strong and fast and have sharp teeth. They use their sense of smell to find prey. They usually hunt the weakest, slowest animal in a group. Wolves are not cruel; they are just good hunters.

Some wolves are near extinction. Their homes are disappearing as people move further into the wilderness. Wolves have also been hunted.

Ranchers and farmers pose another threat to wolves. They become angry when wolves eat their chickens and sheep. This is a serious problem, because the farmers lose their animals, and the wolves are shot by the angry farmers. No one wins in this battle.

Wolves are an important part of the balance of nature. They hunt weak animals and help keep down the populations. In many countries, it is now against the law to hunt wolves. Many zoos and scientists are working hard to protect wolves because they understand just how important wolves really are.

1. Why does the author state that wolves are considered "vicious, evil, and ruthless"?

_____

2. How does the author support the idea that ranchers and farmers are a threat to wolves?

_____

_____

3. The author ends the passage by stating that "wolves are an important part of the balance of nature". Based on the text, what might happen if wolves were to become extinct?

_____

 Reflect

Would the author agree with the statement "There is not anything good to say about wolves"? Use evidence from the text to support your answer.

_____

_____

Read. Then, answer the questions on page 46.

John Adams

The first president to live in the White House in Washington, DC, was John Adams. John Adams was the first vice president of the United States and the second president. When the United States was becoming a country in the late 1700s, John Adams was an important person.

When the country was new, elections for president were different. In today's elections, a presidential candidate chooses a running mate that will become vice president if the team receives the most votes. In the late 1700s, the presidential candidate with the second largest number of votes became vice president. George Washington was the first president, and John Adams was his vice president. When John Adams ran for president in 1796, he had the most votes and Thomas Jefferson had the second most. They made an interesting pair because Jefferson and Adams were **rivals**. They were also friends who respected each other even though they disagreed about many issues.

The 1796 election was the first election to have two political parties: the Federalists and the Democratic-Republicans. John Adams was a Federalist. It was very important to him that the country not fight in a war with the French. The Federalist Party did not last very long past John Adams. The Democrats and the Republicans are the two major parties in the United States now.

Before running for president, John Adams was the head of the committee that wrote the Declaration of Independence. The Declaration of Independence is a written statement that says the United States is its own country, not a colony of Britain. With this statement, the people of the United States no longer would be under the rule of the British King or Britain's laws. They established their own laws and procedures. Americans still celebrate the day the Declaration of Independence was signed on the Fourth of July. John Adams was the leader of the group in Congress that wanted to make the United States an independent country.

John Adams was president for four years. Several years later, his son John Quincy Adams also became president. They were the first father and son to both serve as president. Almost 200 years later, the next father and son presidents were George H.W. Bush and George W. Bush.

John Adams was a great man in US history. He worked hard for the country and spent many years away from his family for his job. That was very difficult for him, but serving his country was extremely important to him.

Name _____

Read the passage on page 45. Then, answer the questions.

1. What was special about the 1796 election?

_____

2. What is the main idea of the passage?

_____

_____

3. What are *rivals*? How do you know?

_____

_____

4. Compare and contrast the election process today to what it was like in the 1700s.

_____

_____

_____

5. The author states that John Adams was an important person. How does the author support this statement?

_____

_____

_____

Reflect

Think about John Adams. What kind of man was he? Use evidence from the text to support your answer.

_____

_____

_____

_____

_____

_____

Read. Then, answer the questions.

Plastic

We use plastic every day. Scientists have worked hard to make it strong and long-lasting. Now, they are finding that plastic is not decomposing and that garbage dumps are filling up. Plastic containers and bags are also polluting beaches and hurting animals. People must be careful about how they throw away plastic.

One thing we can all do is recycle our plastic. Some stores ask customers to return plastic bags. These can be burned because they do not give off poisonous fumes.

Look at the bottom of each plastic container you buy. If it has a recycling symbol with a number in it, you know it can be recycled. If you cannot recycle a container, try to use it for something else.

When you are done with toys or materials made of plastic, try to think of someone else who could use them. Sharing toys and hand-me-downs is a great way to recycle.

Recycling centers sell used plastic to companies that make it into new materials. Recycled plastic can be used to make park benches and timbers for walkways, decks, and even some buildings. Recycled plastic can be made in many colors and is very durable.

Plastic is not a natural material, so it is difficult for it to **decompose** into the earth. For that reason, it is important that we find ways to reuse plastic rather than filling up garbage dumps. What creative ways can you think of to reuse plastic?

1. Why should we look on the bottom of plastic containers?

_____

2. What does *decompose* mean? How do you know?

_____

_____

3. Which text structure does the author use to organize the passage? How do you know?

_____

_____

 Reflect

Why do you think the author uses the word *you* throughout the passage?

_____

_____

_____

Name _____

Read. Then, answer the questions.

Taking Care of Teeth

Long ago, people cleaned their teeth in many interesting ways. They scratched their teeth with sticks, wiped them with rags, or even chewed on crushed bones or shells. Luckily, tooth care has come a long way in the past few hundred years.

It took someone with a lot of time on his hands to invent the first mass-produced toothbrush. In the 1770s, a man named William Addis was in prison. He had an idea to make a tool for cleaning teeth. He used a bone and some bristles from a hairbrush. He carefully drilled holes in one end of the bone. Then, he trimmed the brush bristles and pushed them into the holes. He glued the bristles into place and had the first toothbrush.

People have used different tooth cleaners over the years. Many cleaners, such as crushed bones and shells, actually damaged the protective enamel on teeth. Chalk was a popular cleaner in the 1850s. Baking soda was also used for many years because it was abrasive. Other people used salt as a tooth cleaner. Some toothpastes still contain baking soda and sodium. Fluoride was first added to toothpaste in 1956. It greatly reduced the number of cavities in children. In the 1960s, calcium was added to toothpaste to help strengthen teeth.

Using dental floss once a day is one of the most important things that you can do for your teeth. Originally, floss was made of silk. Now, dental floss comes in different varieties. Dental floss removes "interproximal plaque accumulation," which means that it scrapes off the plaque between your teeth where a toothbrush cannot reach.

The inventions and improvements in dental care have helped people maintain stronger, healthier teeth. We now know how to better care for our teeth every day.

1. What is the main idea of the passage?

_____

_____

2. What is the main idea of the fourth paragraph? What details does the author use to support the main idea?

_____

_____

3. The author uses a chronological text structure in the passage. Underline the evidence in the article that supports this.

 **Reflect**

How has tooth care come "a long way," as the author states?

_____

_____

Name _____

Read. Then, answer the questions on page 50.

Book Review

by Charles Sport

The Zipper Press

Last weekend, as rain dripped from the sky, I read *A Wrinkle in Time* by Madeleine L'Engle. I was transported from a windy autumn night on Earth to planets in galaxies far from ours. The main characters are Meg; her little brother, Charles Wallace; and Calvin, a high school basketball player. They team up with the strange trio of Mrs. Whatsit, Mrs. Who, and Mrs. Which to fight the Black Thing.

A cold shadow lurks as the Black Thing plunges planet after planet into darkness and turns the **inhabitants** into human robots. Meg's father, who has been studying time travel with the US government, is captured by the Black Thing. He is being held on the planet Camazotz. Nearly a year later, his life depends on Meg, a friendless teenager who struggles with schoolwork. Charles Wallace, a six-year-old genius, complicates the rescue when he is taken hostage too.

The three ladies, some of the most delightful characters ever, gave up their lives as stars to battle the Black Thing. Mrs. Whatsit, the youngest, is fond of dressing in wacky earthling clothes. She says to the children, "I didn't mean to tell you. But, oh my dears, I did so love being a star."

Mrs. Whatsit, Mrs. Who, and Mrs. Which whisk the children around space by "wrinkling time." Traveling through time, or tessering, is easy according to Mrs. Whatsit. It seems easy, until Mrs. Which mistakenly lands everyone on a planet that is only two-dimensional. The children flatten like sheets of paper, unable to think or breathe. They are saved moments later by another wrinkle.

To understand wrinkling time, take a sheet of paper and write *present* on the left side and *future* on the right side. Write *time* in the space between. Then, fold the paper so that the two words come together. The present touches the future with no time in between. This is the fifth dimension, or a tesseract, as Mrs. Whatsit calls it. This is a wrinkle in time.

Madeleine L'Engle, who won the Newbery Medal for this book, studied Albert Einstein's theory of relativity. In *A Wrinkle in Time*, she gives kids a peek at time travel without the mind-boggling confusion of advanced math. At one point, Mrs. Whatsit assures Meg that they have taken a "nice tidy wrinkle and they'll be back to Earth five minutes before they left." Unless, of course, "something goes terribly wrong; then it won't matter if they ever get back at all."

A Wrinkle in Time will take you on a wonderful adventure. You will explore unknown worlds, meet interesting characters, and learn about time travel, all from the comfort of your favorite chair.

Name _____

Read the passage on page 49. Then, answer the questions.

1. What award did L'Engle win for *A Wrinkle in Time*?

    _____

2. Is the passage a first- or second-hand account? Circle the evidence in the text that supports your answer.

3. What are *inhabitants*? How do you know?

    _____

    _____

4. What is the main idea of the passage?

    _____

    _____

☀ Reflect

The author discusses the fifth dimension. Based on his description of a tesseract, as well as his description of the book itself, is *A Wrinkle in Time* a good title for L'Engle's book? Use evidence from the text to support your answer.

_____

_____

_____

_____

_____

_____

_____

_____

_____

_____

Name _____

Read. Then, answer the questions.

The Moon

People's first timekeeper was the moon. The wisest men and women in ancient tribes watched the moon's movements in the night sky and carved its progress on rock walls. Their pictures show how the moon "disappears," slowly grows to a full moon, and passes through its phases back to "invisible."

Our ancestors held festivals based on the shape of the moon. They married, danced, and were buried at certain times. The moon needed to be "right."

The light that radiates from the moon is sunlight reflecting off its surface. Only one side of the moon is ever seen from Earth. It appears to change shape because, as it orbits Earth, different parts are lit by the sun. A new moon occurs when the moon is positioned between the sun and Earth. When less than half of the moon is lit, it is called a crescent moon.

In the next phase, the moon is growing. This is called a waxing gibbous moon, which looks like a squashed circle. A full moon occurs when Earth is between the sun and the moon. After the full moon, the lighted portion of the moon is shrinking, or waning. Then the cycle ends and the moon is new again.

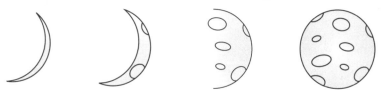

1. What actually causes the moon's light?

   _____

2. The author compares the waxing gibbous moon to a squashed circle. Why is this a good comparison?

   _____

3. The author places the words *disappears* and *invisible* in quotation marks when describing the moon. Why?

   _____

   _____

4. How does the illustration help the reader understand the passage?

   _____

 Reflect

How have the moon's phases been important throughout time?

_____

_____

Name _____

Read. Then, answer the questions.

Ready, Set, Draw!

Many people like to draw, but they do not draw often because they do not think that they are good at drawing. They think that drawing is a magic gift. The truth is, drawing is like any other skill. The more you practice, the better you get.

If you want to learn to draw better, you must first learn to "see." When you start drawing, you will find that you are missing a lot. Most people do not really see what they are looking at. Instead, they see what they think they see.

You can prove this to yourself. First, think about the front of your house. Draw a picture of it. Now, go out and look at the real thing. Count the windows on your drawing and on the front of your house. Did you include all of the features of your house? If you did not, you do not see your house.

Draw a picture of your house while you are looking at it. Notice all of the details. Compare your drawings. Which one is better? Drawing your house while you looked at it probably helped you see it better.

Other good **subjects** to draw are a bowl of fruit, a stack of books, a figurine, or a stuffed animal. Many great artists practice their skills by drawing and painting small objects.

The more you draw, the better you will see. The better you see, the better you will draw. Get some paper and a pencil. Start drawing today!

1. What things must you do if you want to be better at drawing?

_____

2. How does the author prove that most people do not really see what they are looking at when drawing?

_____

_____

3. The author uses the word *subjects* in the passage, but is not referring to school. What is the author referring to? How do you know?

_____

_____

 Reflect

Think about something you are not very good at. What would the author of this passage tell you? Use evidence from the text to support your answer.

_____

_____

Name _____

Read. Then, answer the questions.

The Gravity of Childhood

Sir Isaac Newton was the first person to be able to explain gravity. He was a very important scientist and thinker. But, his life had a rough start. He was born in 1642. His father had just died. His mother married again. Her new husband did not want Isaac. So, the little boy was raised by his grandmother.

When Isaac started school, he was second from the last in his grade! But, he was a good student. He spent much of his time outside. He flew kites and watched how the wind moved them. He observed the clouds and the stars. He was always busy and always thinking.

The hard work paid off. When he left school, he was first in his class. All of the time he spent watching the natural world paid off too. One day, he looked out a window and saw an apple fall from a tree. He wondered why apples always fall to the ground. Why do they not ever fall up or sideways?

That was when Isaac first started thinking about gravity, the force that pulls things toward the earth. It was only one of his important ideas. He also wrote about color and light. Isaac Newton thought of many of his famous ideas during his lonesome but thoughtful childhood.

1. Who raised Isaac Newton?

_____

2. The author states that Isaac's "hard work paid off." How do you know?

_____

_____

3. What lesson can be learned from Isaac's life?

_____

_____

☀ Reflect

Isaac Newton had many important ideas. What character traits led him to think of these ideas? Use evidence from the text to support your answer.

_____

_____

_____

Name _____

Read. Then, answer the questions.

Compost

What happens to your garbage? Not everything you throw away is trash. Some things can be recycled, burned, and composted. A compost pile is a pile of leaves, grass, and leftover foods that you keep outside.

It is not difficult to make a compost pile. All you need is a small corner of your yard or a large wooden box that does not have a top. Other people buy bins that turn the compost for you. You fill the compost with shredded newspaper, grass, leaves, apple peelings, eggshells, and vegetable ends.

You have to take care of your compost pile. If you do not stir it, it can really start to stink. The compost also needs some sunshine and water. If you take care of your compost, the pile will not get any bigger even if you keep adding things to it. A compost pile works in two ways: the sun and water help the leaves, grass, and food leftovers rot and little red worms eat the garbage and turn the food into rich soil. Composted soil works just like **fertilizer**.

A compost pile helps you in a lot of ways. You will have less garbage to throw away, which means that garbage dumps will fill up more slowly. It may also mean that you pay less money for garbage collection. Compost can make very good natural fertilizer. You will be amazed by how quickly the pile gets smaller and by how many critters will live there.

1. List both ways that a compost pile works.

_____

_____

2. What is *fertilizer*? How do you know?

_____

3. What details does the author provide to convince the reader that a compost pile is helpful?

_____

_____

 Reflect

The author uses the word *you* throughout the passage. What impact does this have on the reader?

_____

_____

_____

Name _____

Read. Then, answer the questions.

The *Titanic*

The *Titanic* was one of the finest ships ever built. It was like a floating palace. What was life like on this expensive ship that only sailed on one voyage?

The 329 first-class passengers had cabins with sitting rooms. They could visit with friends in several lounges, restaurants, and dining rooms. They had a gym, a pool, a Turkish bath, a library, and beautiful sunny decks. Their meals were made from the fanciest foods. The passsengers ate at tables decorated with china plates, crystal, and fresh flowers. Everything was even fancier than what most rich people had at home.

The 285 second-class passengers had small, nice cabins. They ate a four-course meal each evening on tables with pretty plates. They could go on deck to walk around or sit in the sun. They did not have restaurants, gyms, and other special rooms. Their decks were smaller because they held the lifeboats.

The 710 third-class passengers had 220 cabins in the noisy rear of the ship. These cabins were used for families. The single men slept in one large room, and the women were in another. The sitting room was a large, plain room with benches and tables. Third-class passengers had to take turns eating. A ticket told them when to eat, and if they missed their times, they went hungry until the next meal.

The passengers knew that they were on a special trip. But, they did not know that the *Titanic* would sink.

1. How many passengers were on board the *Titanic*?

_____

2. Why would third-class passengers make sure to be on time for meals?

_____

_____

3. The author uses a compare/contrast text structure to organize the information. Underline the evidence in the text that supports this.

☀ Reflect

Why do you think the the author ends the first paragraph with a question?

_____

_____

_____

_____

_____

Name _____

Read. Then, answer the questions on page 57.

The Biological Clock

Every living thing has an internal clock. Scientists call it a biological clock. *Bio* means "living." So, you have a living clock. Where is this clock? It is somewhere inside your brain. Unlike your heart, lungs, or kidneys, its location is unknown. Doctors cannot find your clock if it needs to be fixed.

The biological clock is designed to work with the natural cycles of nature. These cycles include day and night, spring and autumn, summer and winter, and the new moon and the full moon. The biological clock ticked away for thousands of years before people invented timekeepers.

Farmers rose every day with the sun to milk the cows and feed the chickens. In the winter, a farming family rested longer hours, often going to sleep with the sunset. By the time the sun reached its peak on the summer solstice in June, the family was working long hours, using every bit of light to their advantage.

The biological clock has a cycle that lasts about 24 hours. It is affected by daylight and darkness. People often feel sick when this clock gets disturbed. Studies have shown that students who stay up late and wake up early to go to school have a harder time remembering what was taught in class than students who went to bed earlier.

Another common problem with a person's clock is something called jet lag. When you fly from one time zone to another, your biological clock can get upset. The more time zones you cross, the more likely you are to develop jet lag.

For example, if you lived in Kansas City, Missouri, and flew with your parents to New York, you would cross only one time zone. You "lose" one hour flying east from Missouri to New York. You might feel that you are not quite as sleepy as you normally are at bedtime, but that is not much of a problem.

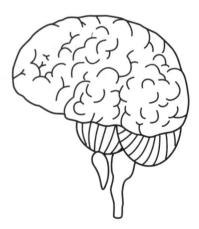

However, if you flew to Paris, France, you would cross seven time zones. Suppose you started your trip at 3:00 pm. The time in Paris would be 10:00 pm when you start. Your trip takes 10 hours, and you land at the airport in Paris at 8:00 am the next morning. The problem is, your biological clock thinks that it is only 1:00 in the morning. Your inner clock is saying, "Go to sleep! Don't wake up!" Your clock has not caught up. It is **lagging behind**.

Because your biological clock is set by sunlight, it is important to follow the natural rhythm of the day when you travel. That first day in Paris will be hard because you will feel very tired. Luckily, a biological clock is not too stubborn. In a few days, it will be on Parisian time!

Name _____

Read the passage on page 56. Then, answer the questions.

1. Where is the biological clock located?

_____

2. What does the clock *lagging behind* mean? How do you know?

_____

_____

3. Explain the purpose of the biological clock.

_____

_____

_____

4. How does the author support the statement that "the more time zones you cross, the more likely you are to develop jet lag"?

_____

_____

_____

☀ Reflect

Based on information from the passage, which problem with the biological clock would be the most difficult? Why?

_____

_____

_____

_____

_____

_____

_____

_____

Read. Then, answer the questions on page 59.

Footprints in the Snow

In 1951, Eric Shipton was climbing Mount Everest, the highest mountain in the world. He and his team were exploring when they saw a scary sight. They saw giant footprints in the snow! It looked as though huge bare feet had made them. Each footprint was about 13 inches (33 cm) long. He said later that it was not the first time he had seen huge footprints like these on Mount Everest.

Eric Shipton was a famous explorer. His pictures of the giant footprints created excitement all over the world. And, there was more to the story. A man named Sen Tensing was one of Shipton's **guides**. Tensing said that he and others had once seen the creature that had made the prints. He said that it was a yeti, or a wild man. This barefoot creature had reddish-brown fur on half of his body. The yeti was more than five feet (1.52 m) tall. Shipton had someone question Tensing about the event. Shipton said that he believed Tensing. The explorer also said that he was sure the footprints were not made by a bear or a mountain ape.

Others were not so sure. Some thought that the huge footprints were made by a bear that lives in the mountains and often walks on two legs. But, Shipton and his men followed the tracks for one mile (1.61 km). Would a bear have walked that far on two legs when it could have run on four? Others say that Tensing saw a mountain ape. But, mountain apes have five toes, and these footprints had only four. Some scientists think that the footprints were made by a smaller animal. Then, the sun melted them so that they looked bigger. Shipton said that the footprints were fresh. Could the sun have had time to melt them? Or, did the explorers really find the footprints of a strange, wild mountain man?

Name _____

Read the passage on page 58. Then, answer the questions.

1. Where did Eric Shipton see the giant footprints?

_____

2. What does *guides* mean? How do you know?

_____

_____

3. What theories does the author provide for the giant footprints?

_____

_____

4. What is the main idea of the passage?

_____

_____

5. How does the illustration help the reader understand the passage?

_____

_____

Reflect

Why does the author end the passage with two questions?

_____

_____

_____

_____

_____

_____

_____

_____

_____

Name _____

Read. Then, answer the questions.

An Accidental Invention

Do you know that many inventions were accidents? Sometimes, new ideas come to people when they are working on something else. Paper towels were invented because of a mistake. The Scott® Paper Company made the first paper towels. They were not out looking for a better towel. The paper towel just showed up at their factory one day.

The Scott Paper Company made toilet paper. They ordered the fine tissue in long rolls from a paper mill. Then, they cut the rolls into the right size and packaged them for home use.

One day, a shipment came from the paper mill that was all wrong. The tissue was too thick and wrinkled. The buyers were ready to send the ruined paper back, when someone had an idea. He said that the thick paper would make nice hand towels that people could use and then throw away.

The Scott Paper Company perforated the rolls of thick paper so that they would tear into towel-sized pieces. They packaged the paper rolls and sold them in stores as "Sani-Towels."

Instead of sending the mistake back, the company created a new product that still sells well more than 100 years later. So you see, mistakes can be great learning experiences if they help you think in new ways.

1. What did the Scott Paper Company originally make?

_____

2. The author states that the "paper towel just showed up." What does the author mean? Use evidence from the text to support your answer.

_____

_____

3. How does the illustration support the information in the passage?

_____

_____

☀ Reflect

What lesson could a reader learn from the passage? Use evidence from the text to support your answer.

_____

_____

_____

Read. Then, answer the questions.

A Mind for New Ideas

Thomas Edison did not stay in school very long. He asked too many questions. After only 12 weeks, his teacher was tired. So, Thomas's mother taught him at home.

Thomas got a job in 1859 when he was only 12 years old. He sold newspapers, candy, and fruit on a train. He built a little laboratory for himself. He did experiments with the telegraph, an exciting new machine. He loved electricity and what it could do.

Thomas received his first patent for an invention at the age of 21. The patent said that Thomas owned his idea and that other people could not copy it. His invention was a voting machine. Then, he started working hard on other inventions. In 1877, he invented something that amazed the world: a phonograph. It played voices and music. Two years later, he invented something even more important. It was a lightbulb.

Soon, Thomas had more than 200 people working for him. He still had a lot of ideas. He invented the battery and the first movie camera. Thomas was not interested in ideas that did not help people.

Thomas Edison created more ideas and inventions for the modern world than any other inventor. He dreamed of a world of light, sound, and movement, and then he made it real.

1. Circle two words in the passage with Greek or Latin roots. What does each word mean?

_____

_____

2. Why is the title a good one for the passage?

_____

_____

3. Describe one of Thomas Edison's character traits. Use evidence from the text to suppport your answer.

_____

_____

 **Reflect**

Reread the last sentence in the passage. How does the author support this statement in the text?

_____

_____

Read the passages on pages 60 and 61. Then, answer the questions.

1. What do both passages have in common?

_____

_____

2. In the article "An Accidental Invention," the author states that many inventions are accidents. Would the author of "A Mind for New Ideas" agree with this statement? Why or why not?

_____

_____

_____

_____

3. Both authors use different text structures to organize the information in the articles. Identify the text structure used in each article. How do you know?

_____

_____

_____

_____

Reflect

"An Accidental Invention" describes the invention of paper towels. Based on what you have read about Thomas Edison, would he have been satisfied inventing paper towels? Why or why not?

_____

_____

_____

_____

_____

_____

_____

_____

Answer Key

Answers will vary but may include the answers provided. Accept all reasonable answers as long as students have proper evidence and support.

Page 5
1. two weeks; 2. first person; Check students' understanding. Words such as *we, us, I, my, me,* and *our* should be circled. 3. to see if the kitten belonged to anyone

Page 6
1. very hungry; 2. She would not let go of the almonds. 3. to help the reader understand how thirsty the raven must be

Page 7
1. decorated; 2. Pay attention to the present so that the future may be what you dream. 3. The girl is daydreaming about dancing, and when she shakes her head, the milk she needed to sell spills.

Page 9
1. Mexico; 2. He wants to be an Air Force pilot. 3. Answers will vary. 4. That evening, they were going to see more of the city's monuments, which looked like shimmering jewels when they were lit at night. It compares the monuments to jewels. 5. Answers will vary.

Page 10
1. He wants a bike and does not have one. He helps Mrs. Benson. 2. If you want something, you will find a way to get it. 3. The bike is old and has flat tires, but Javon thinks it is beautiful.

Page 11
1. almost an hour; 2. She is excited and worried at the same time. 3. She thinks out her idea and presents it to her mom with good reasons and a plan.

Page 13
1. flashed on and off; 2. third person; Words such as *his, he,* and *they* should be circled. 3. Chris could not figure out what was making the light; it was a mystery. 4. his uncle, carrying a flashlight outside checking on the cat in the barn

Page 14
1. suggested; 2. Answers will vary. 3. It would focus on how Uri's music bothers his father and how many problems it causes.

Page 15
1. He is eager to play his new computer game. 2. an accident; 3. Derrick's stomach tightens, his throat tightens, and tears come to his eyes.

Page 16
1. She does not know how to swim and she is going to the beach. 2. She feels excited because she is going to the beach, nervous because she does not know how to swim, happy because she is playing with her best friend, and worried about telling her friend she cannot swim. 3. They are good friends. They do things together and help each other.

Page 18
1. three; 2. first person; Words such as *we, us, our, my, I,* and *mine* should be circled. 3. Phrases such as *the pine trees looked like arrows pointing our way, hear the birds singing and chipmunks moving through the leaves,* and *the water cut through the rock and snaked past flowers and bushes* should be underlined. They help the reader visualize the story. 4. There was no wind blowing through the trees; it was quiet. They could hear everything in the forest. 5. It was family time, and they enjoy family trips. Everything was beautiful, and they stayed and watched the stars together.

Page 19
1. an eye doctor; 2. She can read the board, she has no trouble reading her book, everything is clear, and she likes the way she looks. 3. They are good friends. Rosa helped Penny when she could not see.

Page 21
1. quick, strong; They were able to turn off the motor and sail with only the wind. 2. Phrases such as *they just flopped lightly in the calm air, the wind grew too strong and the waves became large,* and *the cold water was soaking her each time the boat crashed through a wave* should be underlined. 3. the wind; 4. She is brave. She helps her dad in the storm. She is scared. She is shaking from fear. She is helpful. 5. When there is a problem, working together is the best way to solve it. 6. Tina and her father are able to control of the boat and get to safety by working together.

Page 22
1. Someone bought the house. 2. The neighborhood kids love playing games in a fort. When someone bought the house where it was, they talk with the owners to come up with a way they could still play there. 3. Check students' understanding. Phrases that have to do with playing in the fort and talking to the neighbors should be underlined.

Page 23
1. 25 cents; 2. third person; Words such as *they, their,* and *she* should be circled. 3. They need to do this to get the neighbor's attention. If they had not, she might not have bought any lemonade, and the girls might have given up and gone inside.

Page 24
1. Reggie's team had won in overtime. 2. He would feel the tracks rumbling. 3. He heard the train whistle.

Page 26
1. poetry; 2. Students should label things such as the white space, rhyming words, stanzas, lines, the rhyme scheme, and capital letters at the beginning of each line. 3. strong, large; He is a mighty man. His muscles are as strong as iron bands. 4. hearing his daughter sing in the choir; 5. Verses five and six should be circled. The blacksmith is not just strong—he is a good man who loves his family.

Page 28
1. Words such as *frightening, curious, jet-black, crooked,* and *wicked* should be circled. 2. Dreams come at night, but it is hard to remember them once you wake up. Check students' underlining. 3. scared; His heart is beating like a drum and the shadows are "wicked." 4. *my little heart goes a-beating like a drum;* the author's heart and a drum; 5. So that the reader can picture it and hear the noise as it goes up the stairs.

Page 29
1. *Arthur's Nose;* 2. She saved them and told him to draw more. 3. Brown loves drawing and telling stories. His story ideas come from his own life.

Page 30
1. a water clock; 2. The water froze and did not drip. 3. It can be used on cloudy days or indoors, and it could be used repeatedly.

Page 31
1. July 2, 1937; 2. She vanished and there have been no clues found to help figure out why. 3. disappeared suddenly and mysteriously; Phrases such as *was never heard from again, called for a search, try to find the pilot,* and *the search still goes on* should be underlined.

Page 33
1. krill; 2. Some whales are becoming endangered.
3. compare/contrast; The author compares blue whales to sperm whales, talking about their similarities and differences.
4. Answers will vary.

Page 35
1. an engineer; 2. He began writing books for children. 3. Phrases such as *born on November 13, 1850, grew up, 17 years old*, and *1881* should be underlined. 4, His book *Treasure Island* sold out all over Great Britain. 5. It allows us to read some of his poetry for children, supports the main idea of how he wrote for children, and gives examples of his favorite subjects.

Page 36
1. at least one million; 2. with hairs that cover their bodies, organs on their legs, or with the sides of their bodies; 3. Answers will vary.

Page 38
1. He felt it was unfair to people of Jewish or Muslim faith.
2. 1582; 3. a world holiday; the numberless day following December 30; 4. It explains what the United Nations is for readers who may not know. 5. The president did not agree with the World Calendar and did not approve using it. 6. Check students' underlining.

Page 40
1. A firefighter cannot extinguish a fire started by lightning unless it causes a threat to buildings, personal property, or the logging
industry. 2. the possibility of danger; 3. A firefighter must work hard to put out a fire that is started carelessly. A firefighter must carefully watch a natural fire burn and make sure that it does not get out of control. 4. They might use water from lakes and streams, axes to cut away trees, bulldozers to move burnable materials, or an airplane to drop chemicals that slow down fires. They might also light a backfire.

Page 42
1. a horrible event; 2. Yellowstone National Park had a fire that burned over half of the park, but it was a good thing because it allowed a fresh start. 3. New plants grew that were beautiful and are perfect food. Most animals that survived prefer living in the meadows. The heat released some seeds that were trapped in cones. 4. The fire was started by lightning and put out by snow. The author also includes the fact that firefighters could not extinguish the fires.

Page 43
1. About every 300 years, a natural fire can clean up a forest and help make things better. 2. In 1960, firefighters would have had to work very hard to extinguish it immediately rather than letting nature extinguish it. 3. "Managing Fires" is about firefighters and their roles in forest fires. "Yellowstone Fires" is only about the fire at the park in 1988. 4. Answers will vary.

Page 44
1. Fairy tales have led people to belive that wolves are not good, are mean, and hurt people. 2. They shoot the wolves. 3. Animal populations would not be controlled as well.

Page 46
1. It was the first election to have two political parties. 2. John Adams was an important man in US history. 3. people who do not agree or get along; 4. In the 1700s, a person ran for president alone. If he won, he was president. If he came in second place, he was vice president. Today, a presidential candidate chooses a running mate to be vice president if they win. 5. He was head of the committee that wrote the Declaration of Independence and worked hard for the country.

Page 47
1. to see if they can be recycled; 2. to break down into the earth; Students should write phrases such as *long-lasting, garbage dumps are filling up fast*, and *it is difficult for it to decompose back into the earth*. 3. problem/solution; The author talks about the problem that plastic is filling up garbage dumps and gives some solutions, such as looking for recyclable plastic at the store, giving things made of plastic to someone else when you are finished, and recycling.

Page 48
1. There are many inventions that have helped people maintain stronger, healthier teeth. 2. Using dental floss is very important because it removes plaque from between the teeth where a toothbrush cannot reach. 3. Students should underline phrases such as *long ago, now, 1770s, over the years, 1956*, and *most recently*.

Page 50
1. the Newbery Medal; 2. first-hand account; Students should circle words such as *I* and *Book Review by Charles Sport*.
3. people who live in a certain place; Check students' understanding. 4. The author read *A Wrinkle in Time* and thinks that it is a wonderful book that others should read.

Page 51
1. sunlight reflecting off its surface; 2. Only a small part of the moon is lit, so it looks like a circle that has been flattened. 3. The moon has not really disappeared. It is not visible because no sunlight is reflecting off of it. 4. It shows some of the different phases and supports the descriptions of the phases in the text.

Page 52
1. practice, learn to "see"; 2. The author tells you to draw your house from memory. Then, you should compare your drawing to the real thing. There are probably many features you forgot.
3. the main focus of a drawing; Check students' understanding.

Page 53
1. his grandmother; 2. All of the work he did allowed him to be first in his class even though he started at the bottom. 3. If you work hard at something, you will usually do well.

Page 54
1. The sun and water help the leaves, grass, and food leftovers to rot. Little red worms eat the garbage and turn it into soil.
2. a rich material that helps things grow; Check students' understanding. 3. You will have less garbage to throw away, you may pay less for garbage collection, it makes a good fertilizer for your yard, and dumps will fill up more slowly.

Page 55
1. 1,324; 2. If they were late, they went hungry until the next meal. 3. Check students' understanding. They should underline text about the three different levels of tickets and how they were alike and different.

Page 57
1. inside your brain; 2. being behind where it should be; Check students' understanding. 3. Answers will vary but may include that it works with cycles in nature and helps you know when to go to sleep and wake up. 4. by comparing flying across one time zone to flying across seven time zones

Page 59
1. Mount Everest; 2. people who leads others; Check students' understanding. 3. a bear walking on his hind legs, a mountain ape, or the sun melting the ice, making the prints look bigger; 4. Eric Shipton spotted strange tracks. Some people think they may have been caused by a yeti, although no one knows for sure. 5. Answers will vary but may include that it shows what the footprints actually looked like.

Page 60
1. toilet paper; 2. The company did not invent it. It was a mistake that they figured out how to use. 3. It shows what the long roll of tissue looked like.

Page 61
1. Words such as *telegraph* or *phonograph* should be circled. Check students' definitions. 2. Thomas Edison had many ideas that he worked on throughout his life. 3. Answers will vary.

Page 62
1. They are both about inventions. 2. Probably not, because Thomas Edison worked hard at all of his inventions. He thought about each of them and experimented to get them right.
3. "An Accidental Invention" has a problem/solution structure. "A Mind for New Ideas" has a chronological structure. Check students' understanding.